211291620

This book is to be returned on or before
the last date stamped below.

OUR VIOLENT EARTH

STORMS

Fiona Waters

OUR VIOLENT EARTH

STORMS

Other titles in this series:
EARTHQUAKES ● FLOODS ● VOLCANOES

Cover photograph: Lightning over Tucson, Arizona, in the USA.

Title page: A tornado emerges from a spectacular storm cloud in the Midwest of the USA.

Contents page: The 'eye' of Hurricane Linda approaches Mexico in 1997.

This book is a simplified version of the title 'Storms' in Hodder Wayland's 'Restless Planet' series.

Language level consultant: Norah Granger
Editor: Belinda Hollyer   Designer: Jane Hawkins

Text copyright © 2001 Hodder Wayland
Volume copyright © 2001 Hodder Wayland

First published in 2001 by Hodder Wayland, an imprint of Hodder Children's Books.

British Library Cataloguing in Publication Data
Waters, Fiona
Storms. - (Our violent earth)
1.Storms - Juvenile literature
I.Title
551.5'5
ISBN 0 7502 3511 X

Printed and bound in Italy by
G. Canale & C.S.p.A., Turin

Hodder Children's Books
A division of Hodder Headline Ltd
338 Euston Road, London NW1 3BH

Acknowledgements
The publishers would like to thank: Associated Press 4/Dave Martin, 12/Victor R. Caivano, 19/Topi Lyambila, 23/Stefano Sarti, 44/ Dario Lopez Mills; Camera Press 20/Kelly Kerr & Newsmakers, 36/Newsmakers, 38/Vienna Report, 39/Vienna Report, 43 (bottom)/Benoit Gysembergh; Robert Harding 6/Schuster; Impact 17/Javeed A. Jafferji, 43 (top)/Mark Cator; Oxford Scientific Films/Warren Faidley title page, 15, 28; Popperfoto/AFP 35/Yuri Cortez; Popperfoto/Reuters 11/Rick Wilking, 22/Shaun Best, 24/Rafiqur Rahmann, 32/Juan Carlos Ulate; Rex Features 31/Sipa Press, 34; Science Photo Library contents page/NASA & Goddard Space Flight Center, 5/ Gordon Garrard, 26/David Ducros, 27 (both)/David Parker, 29/NASA & Goddard Space Flight Center; Tony Stone Images Cover; 16/Paul Sonders, 25/H. Richard Johnston; Topham 30.
Illustrations Tim Mayer, except pages 18/Nick Hawken; 13 Tony Townsend; 6, 8 (top), 17 (lower), 21/WPL.

Contents

Introducing Storms

NEWS REPORT

Hurricane Georges reached the Gulf of Mexico yesterday as thousands of people were being moved to safety. The fierce winds and torrential rain caused flooding. "The wind is really blowing out there and things are hitting the windows," said Rachel Alonso from a shelter in Gulfport, Mississippi.

Adapted from *The Guardian*,
29 September 1998

What would it be like to be caught in a hurricane? The wind is blowing at over 300 kilometres an hour. Could you survive?

If you were caught outdoors you might survive by climbing into a ditch or lying flat on the ground. This would make it more difficult for the wind to pick you up and throw you around. If you were in a house with a cellar, that would be the best place to go.

Three men struggle through the waves and high winds as Hurricane Georges hits the Florida Keys, in the USA. ▼

Storms happen everywhere in the world. Blizzards hit northern Europe, Asia and America. Hurricanes hurtle across the tropical oceans, and tornadoes spin over the land. This book explains why storms happen, and what scientists can do to try to predict them.

▲ Fork lightning over the town of Tamworth, in New South Wales, in Australia.

What Causes Storms?

Storms happen all over the world, but certain kinds of storm happen more often in some areas than others. Winter blizzards are quite common in the north of Europe, but very unusual in the south. This is because storms are affected by the different climates around the world.

Hot and cold Earth

The different climates on Earth are caused because the middle of the Earth gets more heat from the Sun than the top and bottom, the Poles. At the middle of the Earth, called the Equator, the Sun is right overhead. As you move away from the Equator, the surface of the Earth curves away from the Sun. At the Poles, the Sun's heat is spread over a large area, so it is very cold all year round.

▲ Ice and snow cover the South Pole all year.

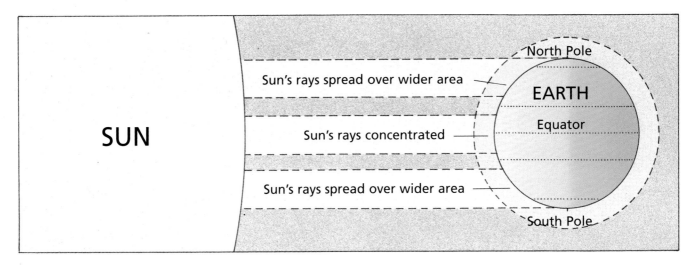

SUN

Sun's rays spread over wider area

North Pole

EARTH

Equator

Sun's rays concentrated

Sun's rays spread over wider area

South Pole

▲ This diagram shows how energy from the Sun reaches different parts of the Earth.

The white snow and ice of the Arctic (North Pole) and the Antarctic (South Pole) reflect a lot of the Sun's heat back into space. But the leafy green rain forests at the Equator absorb the heat. This means the Equator is very hot and the Poles are very cold. This difference in heat makes moving currents of water and wind which take heat from the Equator to the Poles.

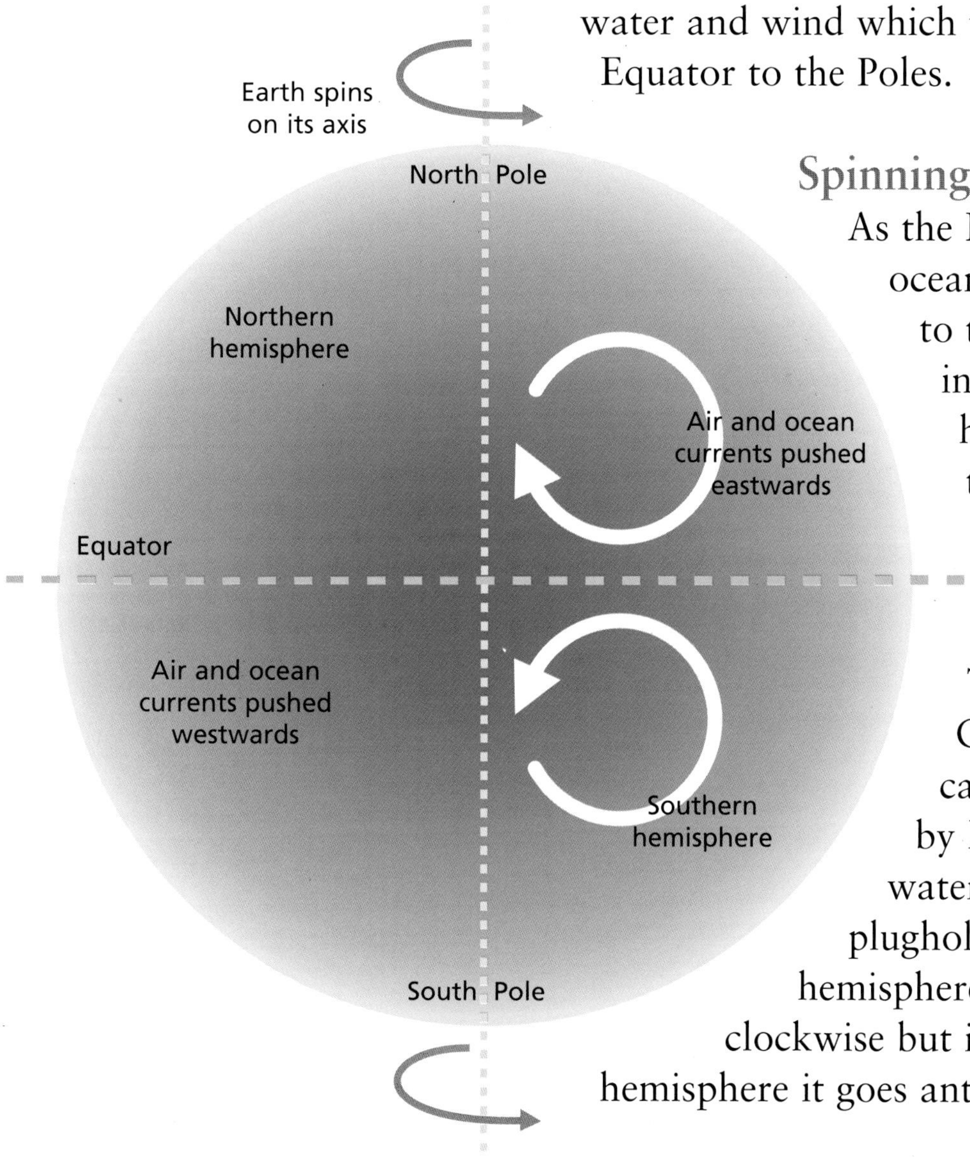

Spinning Earth

As the Earth turns, air and ocean currents are pushed to the right (clockwise) in the northern hemisphere, and to the left (anti-clockwise) in the southern hemisphere. This is called the Coriolis force. You can see this happen by looking at the way water flows down the plughole. In the northern hemisphere it goes down clockwise but in the southern hemisphere it goes anti-clockwise.

Earth spins on its axis

North Pole

Northern hemisphere

Air and ocean currents pushed eastwards

Equator

Air and ocean currents pushed westwards

Southern hemisphere

South Pole

▲ This diagram shows how the spin of the Earth affects the air and ocean currents.

Global climate zones

Equatorial lows

At the Equator, the intense heat from the Sun warms the air. Warm air expands and then rises. As it rises, a space is made below it, and cooler air fills the space. This forms an area of low atmospheric pressure, called the Equatorial lows. The movement of air makes the Trade winds.

Subtropical highs

The hot tropical air which has risen high into the atmosphere cools down as it moves towards the Poles. At a latitude of 30 degrees it is cooler than the air around it, so it sinks. This forms an area of high atmospheric pressure, called the Subtropical highs.

This diagram shows how high and low pressure areas are formed. ▼

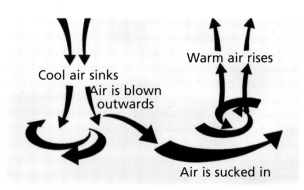

Cool air sinks

Air is blown outwards

Warm air rises

Air is sucked in

▲ High pressure at ground level   ▲ Low pressure at ground level

This map shows some of the winds that flow round the world. Some winds are named after the direction they blow from. Westerlies blow from the west. ▼

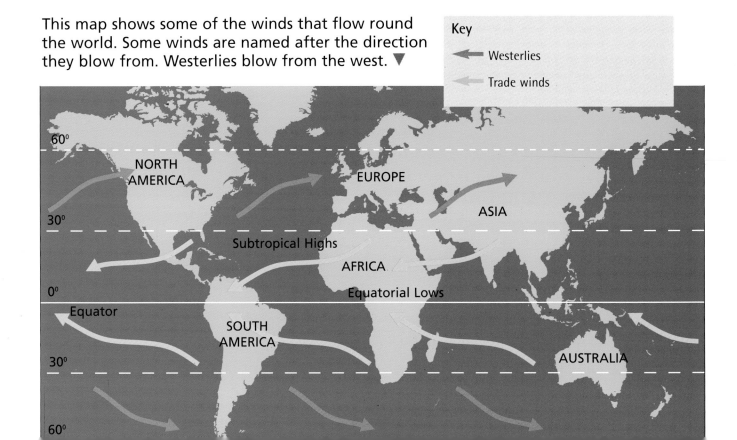

Key

← Westerlies

← Trade winds

60°

NORTH AMERICA

EUROPE

ASIA

30°

Subtropical Highs

AFRICA

0°

Equatorial Lows

Equator

SOUTH AMERICA

30°

AUSTRALIA

60°

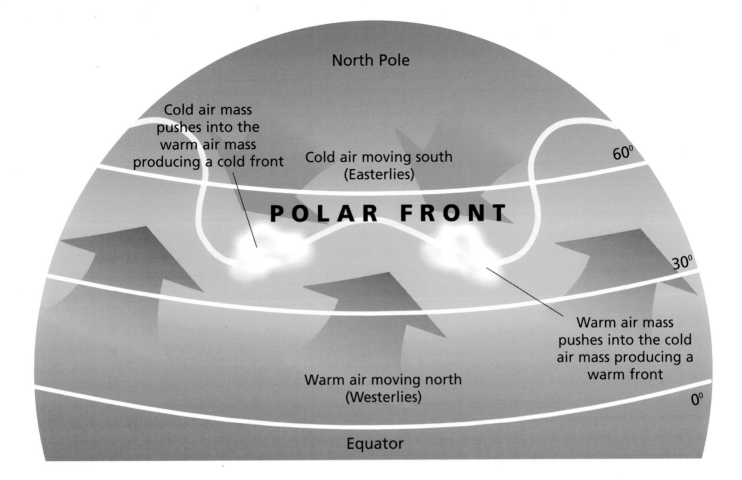

North Pole

Cold air mass pushes into the warm air mass producing a cold front

Cold air moving south (Easterlies)

60°

POLAR FRONT

30°

Warm air mass pushes into the cold air mass producing a warm front

Warm air moving north (Westerlies)

0°

Equator

▲ This diagram shows the cold and warm air meeting at the Polar Front.

Polar Front

There is an area of high pressure at the Poles. The intense cold makes the air super-chilled and it sinks. Cold polar winds called the Easterlies meet the warm, moist Westerlies at the Polar Front. The Westerlies lose a lot of their moisture here, and so rain falls.

Storm zones

Different kinds of storm happen in different climate areas. The main storm zones are:

- the Polar Front where cold dry air meets warm wet air. When the Polar Front is over northern Europe and America during the winter, it causes severe storms and blizzards.

- the Subtropical highs and the trade wind belt. This is where hurricanes begin.

Types of Storm

This map shows the parts of the world most affected by hurricanes. ▼

Hurricanes

The severe storms called hurricanes start in the Atlantic Ocean, the Caribbean Sea, the Gulf of Mexico and the north-east Pacific. In the western Pacific they are called typhoons and in the Indian Ocean and Australia they are called cyclones. Hurricanes, typhoons and cyclones are all the same kind of storm.

Hurricanes start over the oceans. They become less powerful when they move over land. A hurricane begins when the sea temperature is warmer than 26 degrees Celsius as far down as 60 metres below the surface. The air humidity needs to be about 75 to 80 per cent.

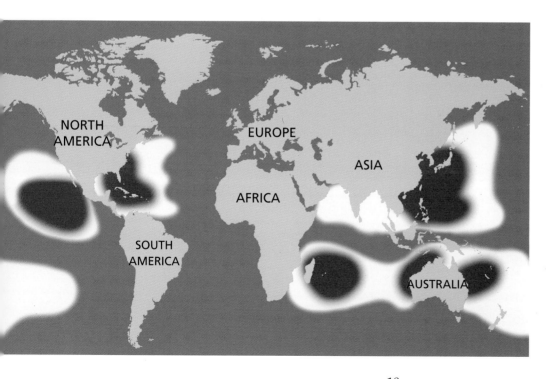

NORTH AMERICA

EUROPE

ASIA

AFRICA

SOUTH AMERICA

AUSTRALIA

Key

☐ Areas at risk from hurricanes

■ Main areas where hurricanes develop

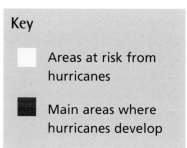

Hurricanes are rare

Hurricanes are quite rare. There are fewer than 50 a year. To be called a hurricane, a storm needs to produce a continuous wind speed of over 120 kilometres an hour. In a big hurricane, the wind speed can be greater than 200 kilometres an hour. A hurricane usually lasts about two or three days.

These people were hit by a huge wave. They were putting boards over their windows to protect them from Hurricane Felix in August 1995. ▼

NEWS REPORT

Up to 700 people are feared drowned after a cyclone hit the coast of Pakistan. Wind speeds of 270 kilometres an hour caused tidal waves which flooded hundreds of fishing villages. Rescue efforts are being delayed by lashing rain.

Adapted from an Associated Press report, 22 May 1999

How does a hurricane develop?

A hurricane begins to form when the warm ocean heats the air above it. Hot air rises, making an area of low pressure. This rising air contains a lot of water vapour that has evaporated from the surface of the ocean. As it rises, it cannot hold as much water vapour. Some of it changes into water droplets, and clouds form.

When the water vapour changes into water it releases heat and makes the air even warmer. This makes it rise higher. The air inside a hurricane can rise 10,000 metres above the ocean. This is the centre of the storm, called the eye.

▲ A house on the coast of Honduras is battered by waves as Hurricane Mitch strikes on 28 October 1998.

When the air inside the hurricane cannot rise any higher, it flows out from the eye. The air gets cooler and falls back to sea-level, where it is sucked back into the centre of the storm. This air that is sucked into the bottom of the hurricane spins the storm.

In the northern hemisphere, hurricanes spin in a clockwise direction. In the southern hemisphere, hurricanes spin in an anti-clockwise direction. This is called the Coriolis effect (see page 7).

66 EYEWITNESS 99

"We were asked to bring an invalid man into the shelter. There were only a few rain squalls at first, but as we loaded the man on to the stretcher, the wind and rain became more violent. We arrived back at the shelter, wet through. Then the electricity failed. We were asked to pick up another man, but we couldn't get out as the rain and winds were too strong."

Paramedic George Metts tells what happened the night Hurricane Hugo hit South Carolina, in the USA, on 21 September 1989. Adapted from a report by the National Oceanic and Atmospheric Administration, in the USA.

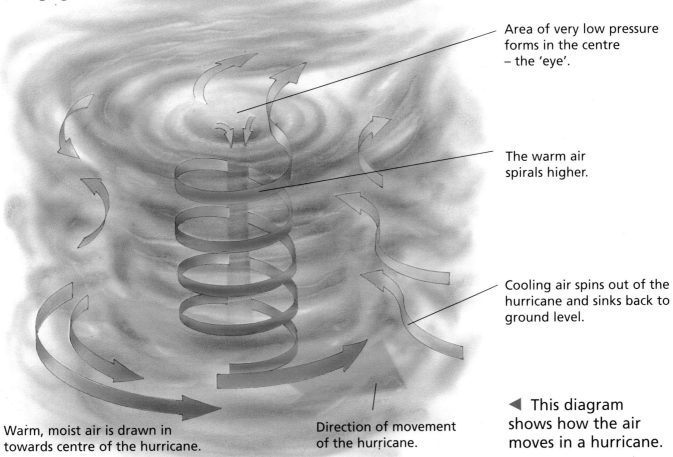

Area of very low pressure forms in the centre – the 'eye'.

The warm air spirals higher.

Cooling air spins out of the hurricane and sinks back to ground level.

Warm, moist air is drawn in towards centre of the hurricane.

Direction of movement of the hurricane.

◄ This diagram shows how the air moves in a hurricane.

DID YOU KNOW?

About 9,000 people have been killed in the USA by tornadoes since 1925.

Tornadoes

A tornado is a violent, spinning column of air. From a distance, the cloud looks like an ice-cream cone. Tornadoes happen most often in the USA. In May, an average of five a day are reported there. In Australia, there are about fifteen a year, They also happen in the UK, Italy, Japan and Central Asia.

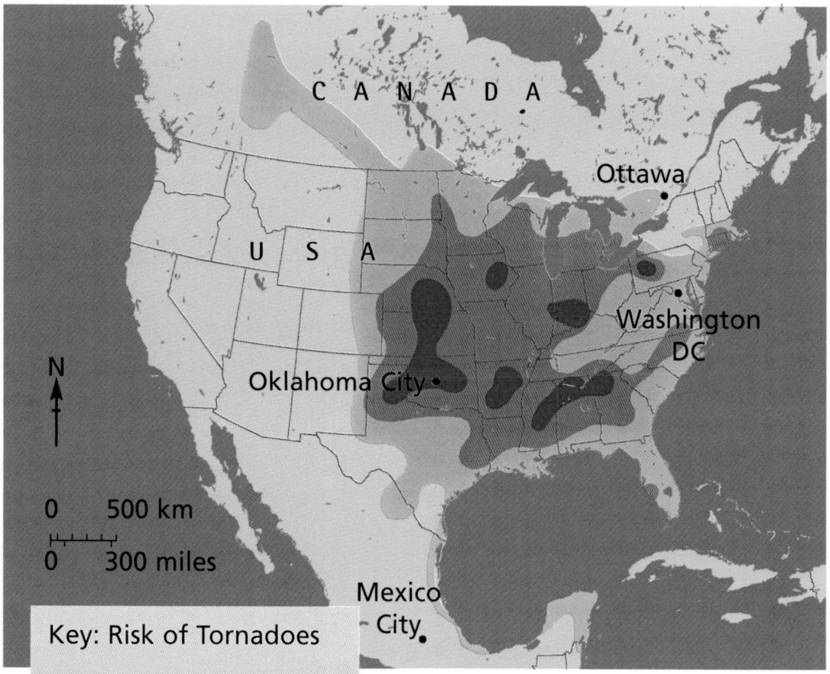

What causes tornadoes?

Tornadoes usually form over land rather than water. In late spring and early summer over the Great Plains of the USA, the Sun heats the ground and warm, moist air rises. As it rises, it cools and forms large clouds. The air around is sucked into the tornado.

Key: Risk of Tornadoes

Medium risk

High risk

Highest risk

▲ This map shows the areas most at risk from tornadoes in North America.

Measuring tornado strength

The Fujita (F) Scale measures the tornado by the speed at which it spins. Tornadoes described as F1 are usually (but not always) harmless. F4 and F5 tornadoes are very scary. But usually there are only two F5 tornadoes a year in the USA. They usually only reach F5 for a few seconds. An F6 tornado is possible, but nobody has ever recorded one.

▲ The great cloud of dust and debris from a tornado in the USA.

FUJITA SCALE

Fujita scale	Spinning speed (kph)	Effects
F0 (weak)	Less than 116	Minor damage to buildings and trees.
F1 (weak)	117–180	Minor damage to buildings and trees.
F2 (strong)	181–253	Vehicles pushed off roads, roofs torn off buildings.
F3 (strong)	254–331	Vehicles lifted off ground, severe damage to weaker buildings, e.g. wooden houses.
F4 (violent)	332–418	Vehicles picked up and carried over 2 km, wooden and brick buildings destroyed.
F5 (violent)	419–512	Many buildings destroyed, depending on size of tornado.
F6 (extreme)	More than 512	Total devastation – nothing left standing.

 A mountaineer caught in a blizzard tries to protect himself.

Winter storms

Rain, ice, wind, hail and snow are all common at the Polar Front in the winter. The worst storms are called blizzards. Temperatures fall as low as -12 degrees Celsius, and you can only see a few metres in front of you.

At the Polar Front in the northern hemisphere, warm air from the subtropics meets cold polar air. Waves develop where these air masses meet, and make a warm front and a cold front.

The same thing happens in the southern hemisphere. The warm air is chilled, clouds develop, and rain, snow or hail may form. The air temperature must be below 4 degrees Celsius for snow to fall on the ground.

Monsoons

The monsoon belt lies across southern Asia and part of central Africa. The land becomes very hot in summer, and warm air rises. This forms an area of low pressure. Moist air is sucked in, and as this air rises the moisture falls as torrential rain.

Monsoons can cause terrible floods. But they are also a vital supply of water in Asia and central Africa. About 40 per cent of the world's population live in the monsoon belt. People need monsoons for their crops.

▲ Two boys shelter from the rains on the island of Zanzibar.

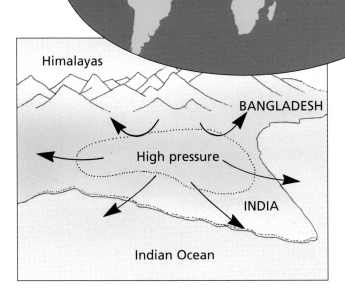

◄ This map shows the area where there are monsoons.

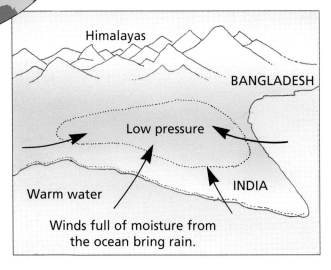

▲ 1. The land is cold in winter. Sinking dry air causes high pressure. Winds blow outwards.

▲ 2. The land heats up in the summer. Rising warm air causes low pressure. Monsoon rains are sucked in by warm air.

The El Niño Effect

Every few years the world's weather is affected by El Niño. El Niño is Spanish for 'The Boy Child', which means Jesus. This is because the change in the weather is often around Christmas time.

What is El Niño?

El Niño is a change in air pressure. Normally, there is an area of low pressure over the western Pacific where the warm water heats the air above it. As the warm, moist air rises, more air is dragged across the Pacific. These strong air currents are the trade winds. They pull the water on the surface away from the coast of South America, and towards the centre of the Pacific.

When El Niño arrives, the low pressure area moves closer to South America. The trade winds become weaker. This change in the flow of air across the ocean changes the direction of the jet stream. It brings stormy weather to areas far from the Pacific.

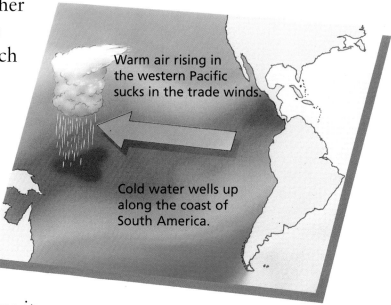

Warm air rising in the western Pacific sucks in the trade winds.

Cold water wells up along the coast of South America.

▲ 1 This diagram shows normal conditions in the Pacific Ocean.

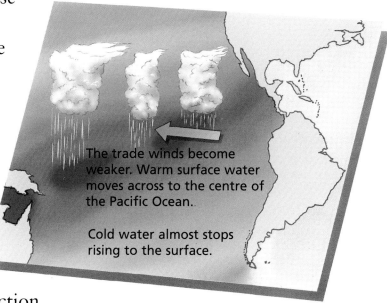

The trade winds become weaker. Warm surface water moves across to the centre of the Pacific Ocean.

Cold water almost stops rising to the surface.

▲ 2 This diagram shows the changes caused by El Niño.

La Niña

The climate in the Pacific usually swings from normal to warmer El Niño conditions. Sometimes it goes the other way, from normal to colder conditions. This is called La Niña, which is Spanish for 'Little Girl'.
El Niño and La Niña are like two ends of a seesaw.

What does El Niño do?

El Niño brings floods to some areas and droughts to others. The El Niño that happened in 1982–3 was the strongest ever recorded. There were droughts in Africa and Australia. But in Peru, which normally has 250 milimetres of rain in a year, there were 2 metres instead. El Niño might also affect the way hurricanes develop.

▲ Parts of Kenya were flooded in 1998. People thought this was because of El Niño.

NEWS REPORT

For about two weeks, torrential rain has been falling in California, killing at least nine people. Rivers have burst their banks and mudslides have buried cars. Skiers are delighted because the Sierra Nevada has received more than twice the normal snowfall for this time of year.
What's wrong with the weather? What's wrong with it is El Niño.

Adapted from *Earth: The Science of Our Planet*, January 1995

Storm Hazards

Wind damage

Storms can damage buildings in many ways. High-speed winds can tear off roofs, and even blow down buildings. In a severe hurricane or tornado, cars and trees can be picked up and hurled at buildings. Glass from broken windows flies through the air, making a cloud of sharp pieces.

A lot of damage can also be caused by the difference in pressure inside a building and the storm outside. In the eye of a hurricane the pressure outside can be lower than the pressure inside. This makes buildings explode outwards.

This building in Oklahoma, in the USA, collapsed in a tornado on 4 May 1999. ▼

Lightning

Lightning happens when thunderstorms bring together positive electrical charges at the top of clouds, and negative charges at the bottom. When the difference between the charges at the top and bottom of the cloud is great enough, there is a sudden electrical burst. This burst is a lightning strike. It lasts only millionths of a second. The high temperature of the strike causes the flash and the thunderclap.

DID YOU KNOW?

In the USA, about 130 people die each year after being struck by lightning.

These diagrams show how lightning happens. ▼

Lightning can have four main effects:

- people and animals can be killed
- material struck by lightning can be burnt up
- the high temperature can start fires
- sudden bursts of power can damage electrical equipment.

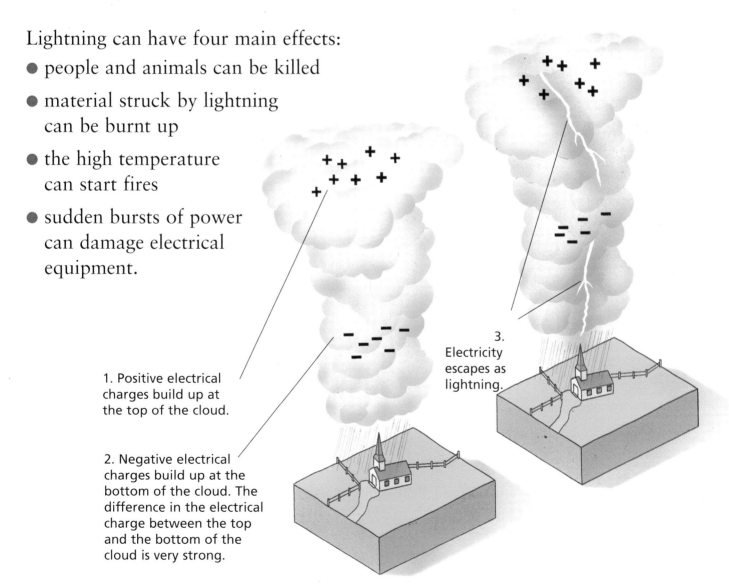

1. Positive electrical charges build up at the top of the cloud.

2. Negative electrical charges build up at the bottom of the cloud. The difference in the electrical charge between the top and the bottom of the cloud is very strong.

3. Electricity escapes as lightning.

The weight of ice on top of this traffic light in Montreal, in Canada, has made it bend over. ▼

Hail, snow and ice

Hail and snowstorms can cause great damage to crops and trees, and to powerlines and buildings. In the USA, $760 million-worth of damage is caused every year by hail and snowstorms. Two per cent of the country's crops are destroyed. In January 1998, ice-storms brought down thousands of powerlines in Canada. Millions of people were left without any heat in freezing weather.

 DID YOU KNOW?

When Hannibal crossed the Alps in 218 BC to invade Rome, he had 40,000 soldiers. Blizzards killed 16,000 of the soldiers.

Avalanches

Avalanches happen when snow builds up on slopes, and then falls without warning. Snow cannot build up on very steep slopes, and snow cannot fall downhill on gentle slopes. But avalanches are a real danger on slopes that are at a fairly steep angle. Millions of tonnes of snow can rush downhill at over 320 kilometres an hour, crushing everything in the way.

▲ Houses in the small Italian village of Morgex were smashed by an avalanche on 23 February 1999.

DID YOU KNOW?

The fastest avalanche ever was measured in Switzerland in 1898. It reached 349 kilometres an hour.

There are about 100,000 avalanches a year in the American Rocky Mountains, but most are in areas where people do not live. As skiing and snowboarding become more popular, more people are at risk from avalanches. In February 1999, 38 people were killed by an avalanche in Galtür, in Austria.

Avalanches can kill people in three ways. When the snow rushes downhill, it picks up rocks and soil which can crush a person. People buried under snow can suffocate very quickly, or die from the cold.

NEWS REPORT

The floods in Bangladesh are killing people through drowning, electrocution and even snake bites. You have to carry metal jars hundreds of metres to the nearest hand pump to get safe drinking water. In the streets of Gulshan, people have managed to stay on in their homes by piling their beds and tables above the water level. So they are living squashed right up against the corrugated iron roofs.

Adapted from *The Independent*,
7 September 1998

Floods

Floods can cause billions of pounds of damage, and many deaths. In 1998, monsoon rains caused serious flooding in Bangladesh. Over 60 per cent of the country was covered by floodwater. It poured through the homes of more than 30 million people. Floods in China were made even worse by a hurricane. People live on flood plains because the land is good for farming, but stormy weather can bring disaster to these areas.

People queue to collect clean drinking water in Dhaka, the capital of Bangladesh. ▼

Flash floods happen when slow-moving thunderstorms bring heavy rain over a particular area. When this happens, over 50 millimetres of rain can fall in an hour. The ground becomes so full of water that it cannot hold any more.

Melting snow can also cause flash floods hundreds of kilometres from the snowfall. In February 1999 there was a sudden thaw after severe snowstorms in the Alps. This caused serious flooding in parts of Germany and Switzerland. Flash floods cause a lot of damage because there is very little warning, but also because they carry lots of mud and debris along in the water.

▲ Storm waves batter the coastline of France.

Coastal erosion and storm surges

Storms are the main cause of erosion along coasts. Heavy rain soaks the ground, which makes cliffs weaker and more likely to fall down. Stronger winds make the waves higher along the coastline. These waves can be so high that they form a storm surge which floods the land. As the water is sucked back into the sea, it erodes the coast.

 DID YOU KNOW?

In January 1999, there were three weeks of heavy rain. Erosion by the sea caused a huge rock fall at Beachy Head in Sussex, in England. Around 50,000 tonnes of rock fell from the cliffs in one day.

Predicting Storms

Scientists know that certain types of storm happen in certain areas. The climate of an area is the usual pattern of weather over at least thirty years. To predict storms, scientists need to know how weather changes from day to day. Scientists who predict and measure the weather are called meteorologists.

Measuring the weather

Weather data is collected by satellites, balloons, aircraft and weather stations on the ground and at sea.

Meteorologists use this data to check the changes in temperature, atmospheric pressure and cloud cover. Then they can predict the weather for the next few days or weeks.

◀ This weather satellite is watching the weather over Europe and Africa.

Chaos Theory

It is difficult to predict the weather, and forecasts are often wrong. But there are reasons why weather is so hard to predict. Very small changes in the atmosphere can have unusual or 'chaotic' effects on weather patterns. They can change the strength or direction of a hurricane, for example. This is called Chaos Theory. Another name for this is the Butterfly Effect, because changes as small as the flapping of a butterfly's wings can have a great effect on the weather.

▲ A meteorologist transfers data recorded by an automatic weather station on to his own computer.

Meteorologists never know which of the small changes in weather will happen together, and cause a great change. They can predict usual patterns, such as May being the worst month for tornadoes in the USA. But they cannot tell exactly when or where a tornado will happen. Even with detailed data and computers, they cannot be sure about the weather for more than two days ahead.

◄ This weather balloon measures wind speeds, temperature and humidity.

Predicting hurricanes

Weather satellites are the most important instruments used to track hurricanes. There are two types. Polar orbiting satellites spin around the Earth from Pole to Pole. Geostationary satellites stay in the same position above the Earth all the time. These satellites track rain clouds to see if they change into a hurricane.

A hurricane's path

Once a hurricane forms, it is vital to know when and where it will reach land, so people can be moved to safety. In most cases, meteorologists can predict the path of a hurricane up to 24 hours in advance. Very detailed data and huge computer models can be used, but even they do not always get it right. Hurricane Mitch is an example of when it went wrong (see pages 32–35).

Hurricane warnings

Meteorologists know that a hurricane may change course at the last moment. This is why warnings are given just 12 to 18 hours before the hurricane reaches land.

MONTAGE OF GOES-8 INFRARED IMAGES FROM HURRICANE GEORGES FROM 18-28 SEP 1998 NEAR 12 UT

▲ This computer image shows the path of Hurricane Georges across the southern states of the USA from 18–28 September 1998.

A 3-D computer image of Hurricane Linda off the coast of Mexico in 1997. The hole in the centre is the 'eye' of the storm. ▶

Famous Storms

Hurricane Gilbert, 1988

Hurricane Gilbert hit Jamaica on 12 September 1988. It was one of the worst storms ever recorded in the Caribbean. Wind speeds reached 150 kilometres an hour, with gusts of 225 kilometres an hour. After Jamaica, the hurricane moved to Mexico, where 200 people were killed.

As Jamaica is often in the path of hurricanes, a lot of work had been done to move people to safety. Only a few people died, but the real problem was the effect on people's jobs. The cost of the damage was 3,000 million dollars. Hurricane Gilbert proved that even with advance warning, a really big storm will cause a great deal of damage.

▲ This house in Jamaica was hit by a falling tree.

This map shows the path of Hurricane Gilbert across the southern USA and the Caribbean. ▼

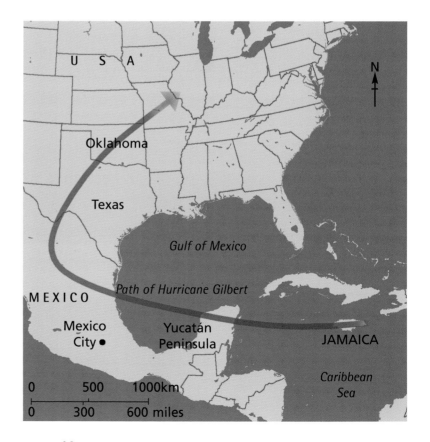

▲ This ship was
washed ashore
in Mexico by
Hurricane Gilbert.

The damage

One in every four houses in Jamaica was damaged.
The roof was ripped off a church where 400 people
were sheltering. Most of the 580 schools were
damaged. Ten of the hospitals were damaged just
when they were most needed. The roof was blown off
the main telephone exchange and the rain destroyed
the switchboard, so all the telephone lines were cut.
Radio and television masts were blown down by the
winds. This made it difficult to organize the rescue
effort. There was a lot of damage to crops and
industry, but over 40 per cent of businesses had
insurance.

Lessons learnt

Before Hurricane Gilbert, many roofs were made from
very cheap aluminium sheeting. The strong winds
blew this metal away from its fixings. The law has
now been changed, and all new buildings must be
able to survive a hurricane without serious damage.

Hurricane Mitch, 1998

On 28 October 1998, Hurricane Mitch hit Central America. It was the worst hurricane in 200 years, with winds of 290 kilometres an hour and 60 centimetres of rain falling every day. The people were not prepared for the disaster. We do not know how many people were killed because many bodies still lie buried under metres of mud. But we think that over 20,000 people were killed, and about two million were made homeless.

 EYEWITNESS

"I have seen earthquakes, droughts, two wars, cyclones and tidal waves. But this is the worst thing I have ever seen."

Cardinal Miguel Obando y Bravo of Managua, Nicaragua, quoted in *The Independent*, 4 November 1998

People from El Progreso in Honduras try to reach their homes. ▼

NEWS REPORT

Jerry Jarrell, the director of the National Hurricane Centre in Miami, in the USA, said that the usual method of predicting hurricanes had let them down this year. "It predicted the winds, but not the rainfall," Mr Jarrell said. A new system should predict how much rain a hurricane would carry. Poor communications had also made the disaster worse.

Adapted from *The Independent*, 2 December 1998

This map shows how Central America was affected by Hurricane Mitch. ▼

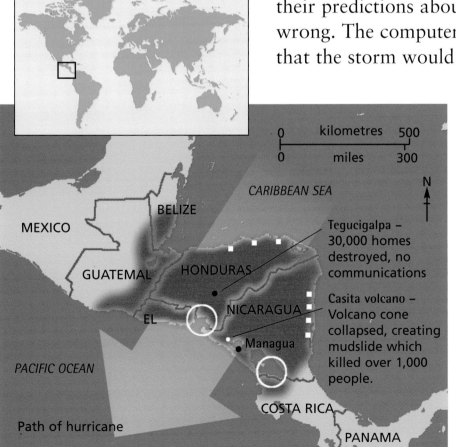

The National Hurricane Center and the Hurricane Research Center both say that their predictions about Hurricane Mitch were wrong. The computer models had predicted that the storm would turn west, but it turned south and hit Central America. Scientists think they did not properly work out what effect El Niño would have on the hurricane.

Tegucigalpa – 30,000 homes destroyed, no communications

Casita volcano – Volcano cone collapsed, creating mudslide which killed over 1,000 people.

Key

☐ Towns and villages cut off

◯ Very severe floods

■ Farmland destroyed

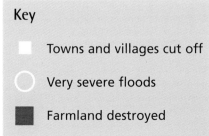

The damage

The worst-hit country was Honduras, which has a population of nearly 6 million people. About 85 per cent of the country was under flood water. The River Hamuya, which usually flows quietly and is 60 metres wide, was a torrent, 500 metres wide. Over 100 bridges, 80 per cent of the roads, and 75 per cent of the country's agriculture were destroyed. Most of the banana plantations were lost. The total repair bill after Hurricane Mitch will be over $2 billion.

Laura Arriola de Guity was rescued by a helicopter crew who spotted her far out at sea. ▼

Lessons learnt

The most important lesson of Hurricane Mitch is that poor countries do not have the money or equipment to cope with natural disasters. For example, the government of Nicaragua did not have enough money for fuel for the rescue helicopters.

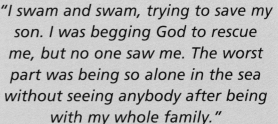

66 EYEWITNESS 99

"I swam and swam, trying to save my son. I was begging God to rescue me, but no one saw me. The worst part was being so alone in the sea without seeing anybody after being with my whole family."

Laura Arriola de Guity was swept out to sea by the floods that hit Honduras. She was found six days later, 120 km from her home. All her family was killed.

The other important lesson of Hurricane Mitch is that the international relief agencies and foreign governments must help faster. Without food or medical help, starvation and disease spread rapidly. It took weeks for aid to reach people. Poor countries cannot pay for aid themselves. Other countries have given $100 million in aid, but $5 billion is needed to rebuild Central America.

These houses in Tegucigalpa, the capital of Honduras, were destroyed by Hurricane Mitch on 3 November, 1998.

Tornado Alley, USA

Tornado Alley stretches across the Midwest of the USA. Here, warm air from the Gulf of Mexico meets cold, dry air from the north. This causes huge thunderclouds, and these can create tornadoes.

Oklahoma, 1999

On 4 May 1999, the US states of Kansas and Oklahoma were hit by the fiercest tornadoes for ten years. 43 people were killed and 700 injured as 40 separate tornadoes struck. A wind speed of 511 kilometres an hour was recorded. Paving stones were ripped up, and $800 million-worth of damage was caused in Oklahoma City alone.

 DID YOU KNOW?

On 18 March 1925, a tornado raced across Missouri, Illinois and Indiana, in the USA, at over 80 kilometres an hour. It killed 695 people.

A teenager in the wreckage of his home after it was hit by a tornado in May 1999. ▼

'Terrible Tuesday'

On Tuesday 3 April 1974, the worst tornadoes in the USA happened. 148 tornadoes touched down in twelve states. At least 300 people were killed, and over 5,000 injured.

Chasing tornadoes

The National Severe Storms Laboratory in Oklahoma is right in the centre of Tornado Alley. Scientists from here chase tornadoes to try to learn more about them. They know what causes tornadoes, but they do not yet know how to tell when a severe thunderstorm will turn into a tornado. Once they know the answer to this question, they will be able to warn people when a tornado is coming.

▲ This dramatic photograph is of a tornado in the Midwest of the USA.

❝ EYEWITNESS ❞

"I was working that day as a forecaster for the National Weather Service in Louisville, Kentucky. Half an hour after the tornado warning, we saw a thunderstorm approaching. We could see the funnel cloud forming. Suddenly, an instrument shelter that had been bolted to the roof fell in front of our window. This was one of 148 twisters. It was the first tornado I ever saw."

John Forsing describes what happened on Terrible Tuesday, 3 April 1974. Adapted from a report by the National Oceanographic and Atmospheric Administration, USA.

Alpine snowstorms, 1999

In February 1999 the European Alps were hit by the heaviest snowfalls in living memory. Road and rail links were cut, and thousands of tourists were stranded. Because the snowfall was so sudden and so heavy, many avalanches were set off, and over 70 people were killed.

 EYEWITNESS

"We were drinking mulled wine when it started. The lights went out. There was only dust and snow. We got out of there as fast as we could."

Franz Wekno, a hotel owner in Galtür, Austria

Avalanche in Austria

The worst avalanches were in the Paznaun valley in Austria, in the villages of Galtür and Valzur. The villages were not protected by avalanche barriers and 38 people were killed.

Rescuers looking for survivors of the avalanche in Galtür, Austria. ▼

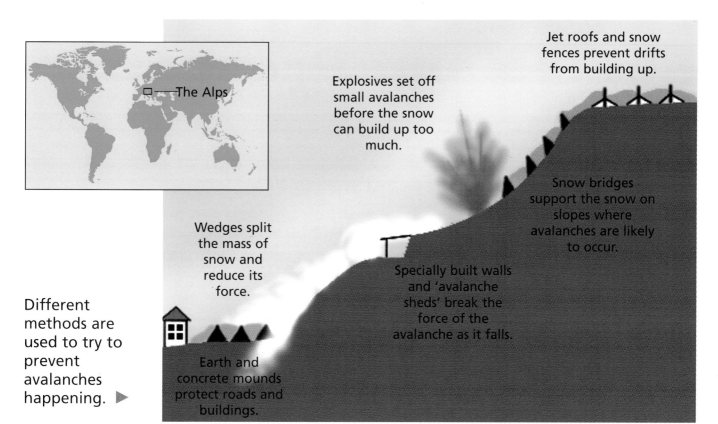

The Alps

Jet roofs and snow fences prevent drifts from building up.

Explosives set off small avalanches before the snow can build up too much.

Snow bridges support the snow on slopes where avalanches are likely to occur.

Wedges split the mass of snow and reduce its force.

Specially built walls and 'avalanche sheds' break the force of the avalanche as it falls.

Earth and concrete mounds protect roads and buildings.

Different methods are used to try to prevent avalanches happening. ▶

NEWS REPORT

Holidaymakers and locals grabbed torches and organized rescue parties. Unfortunately, the emergency equipment had been stored at the fire station which lay right in the path of the avalanche. In the few hours when it really mattered, the lifesaving tools were buried under tonnes of snow.

Adapted from *The Independent on Sunday*, 28 February 1999

The snow drifts were so deep that the only way in and out of the valley was by helicopter. The weather stopped the rescue squads from getting to the area until 16 hours after the avalanche. Villagers had spent the night digging with their bare hands to find people buried below tonnes of snow.

Lessons learnt

On this occasion the snowfall was very sudden and heavy. In areas not usually at risk from avalanches there was little that could have been done to prevent the disaster. Only a few people were killed out of all those who were in the area. So people living and holidaying in the Alps are generally well-protected.

Rescue and Prevention

▲ Rescue workers find a person trapped under the snow.

Rescue and relief plans

Storms and other natural disasters will always happen. More research will help scientists to predict when and where storms will hit. But governments and rescue agencies must plan for the worst.

After a storm, people who are trapped must be rescued quickly. People buried in avalanches can die within 30 minutes. When a building collapses in a hurricane, less than half the people trapped will still be alive after six hours. Rescuers first try to rescue people who have a good chance of living if they get medical help quickly. They have to leave until last the people who are so badly hurt they may die, and people who are not badly hurt.

The biggest problem is that rescue efforts need to start while the storm is still happening. During the 1999 snowstorms in the Alps, the roads were closed because of the heavy snow, and the weather was too bad for helicopters.

66 **EYEWITNESS** 99

"We could have started the airlift 30 minutes after the avalanche, but we were stopped by the bad weather."

Wendelin Weingartner, the governor of Tyrol province in Austria, January 1999

Relief and Rescue Plan

1. Assess overall damage

2. Immediate rescue of trapped people

3. Provide medical assistance from outside the area

4. Assess human need for food, water and shelter

5. Distribute emergency aid

6. Assess condition of buildings and bridges, pull down dangerous structures

7. Restore communications and start up businesses again

8. Begin rebuilding using storm-resistant material

9. Start programme of storm education

Disease

One of the biggest problems after a big natural disaster is the spread of disease. If disease is not prevented, it can kill as many people as the storm itself. After Hurricane Mitch, diseases like cholera spread because there were so many unburied bodies. People could not find fresh water or get medical supplies.

Mitigation and education

Efforts to reduce the damage caused by storms are called mitigation. Point nine on the Rescue and Relief Plan (left) is about storm education. After a storm, the authorities might need to bring in stricter laws on how buildings are put up. People need to be taught what to do when a storm is coming.

Reducing poverty

It is much harder for poor countries to recover after a storm. In Nicaragua, for example, only 58 per cent of the people had a fresh water supply before Hurricane Mitch struck. After the hurricane it was much worse. More than a third of the people cannot read or write. This makes it difficult to organize storm education plans. Poor countries usually owe millions of dollars to the richer nations. This means they do not have the money to repair the damage caused by storms.

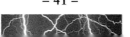

The Future

Global warming

Carbon dioxide and water vapour in the atmosphere cause a natural 'greenhouse effect'. This raises the temperature of the Earth's surface so it is warm enough for life to exist. But over the last 150 years carbon dioxide, methane and nitrous oxide have been pumped into the atmosphere by industry. This has made temperatures on Earth rise. This is called global warming.

▲ A new office block twisted by the hurricane that hit Britain in 1987.

Stronger storms

Scientists think that global warming is making storms happen more often. In 1995, the surface of the Atlantic Ocean was hotter than usual, and at the same time there were eleven hurricanes and nineteen tropical storms. This is double the usual number in a year.

NEWS REPORT

At least six people were killed by a sudden storm in Moscow on Saturday night. The gale, or uragan, occurred after two weeks of very hot weather with temperatures above 30 degrees Celsius. The mayor has blamed meteorologists for not warning people about the uragan.

Adapted from *The Guardian*, 22 September 1998

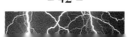

Global warming is likely to make storms even more difficult to predict. This is very serious for the millions of people living in the monsoon area. They need regular monsoon rains for life-giving water. If the difference in temperature between the northern and southern hemispheres changes even a little, it will affect the monsoons. It will bring drought in some areas and terrible floods in others.

DID YOU KNOW?

The normal yearly temperature has risen steadily since 1980, and 1997 and 1998 were the hottest years on record.

These floods in China in 1998 came after an unusually heavy monsoon. ▼

El Niño and global warming

El Niño (see pages 18-19) usually happens every three to seven years. Since 1991, it has returned in 1991–2, 1992–3, 1994–5 and 1997–8. Some scientists think this is because of global warming.

Scientists have worked out the surface temperature of the Pacific Ocean for the last 200 years. This has shown that El Niño returned about every five years. But over the last forty years, El Niño has happened about every three years. La Niña, the time when the ocean is cooler than normal, has been happening less often. Maybe global warming is making the oceans warmer, so El Niño happens more often.

◀ A rain forest burning in Brazil in 1998. The usual seasonal rains did not arrive, probably because of El Niño. This meant it was easy for fires to spread through the very dry forest.

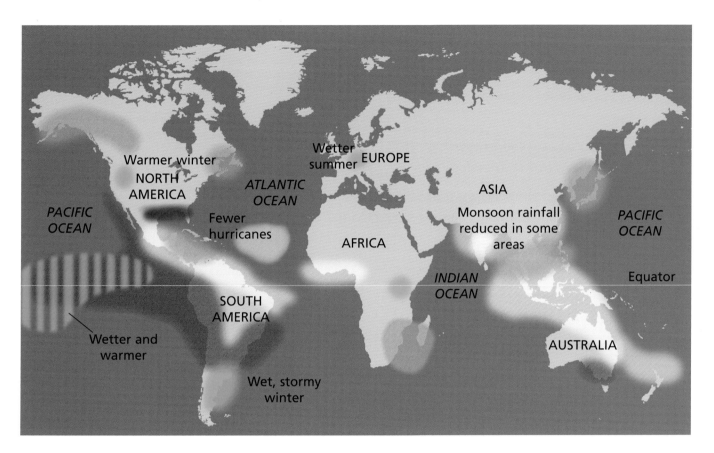

▲ This map shows the areas of the world that had changes in their usual climate during 1998. Many scientists believe these were caused by El Niño.

Key

The effects of El Niño

- Dryer
- Warmer
- Dryer and warmer
- Dryer and cooler
- Wetter
- Wet and cool winter

In 1997–98, El Niño was the strongest on record. There were droughts in the southern USA, East Africa, northern India, north-east Brazil and Australia. In Indonesia, forest fires burned out of control, making a thick smog which spread into countries nearby.
In California, parts of South America, the Pacific, Sri Lanka and east central Africa there were torrential rains.

Will El Niño and global warming lead to more storms in the future? Scientists cannot tell yet, but they do know that storms are the most frightening natural forces on the planet.

Glossary

atmospheric pressure The amount of air that is pressing down on the earth.

avalanche The fast fall of large quantities of snow, mud and rocks down a steep slope.

blizzard A severe winter storm with driving snow and strong winds.

cirrus cloud High white cloud in long wispy strands.

climate Weather conditions in different parts of the world.

Coriolis force The way in which air and ocean currents are forced east or west.

cyclone A violent wind storm.

El Niño The change in pressure that makes the trade winds weaker and sends warm water towards South America.

equator The imaginary line that runs round the middle of the earth.

erosion The wearing away of rock and soil by the wind or water.

Fujita Scale The system of describing tornadoes by their wind speed, and the amount of damage they will cause.

hemisphere Half of the Earth. The northern hemisphere is above the Equator, the southern hemisphere is below.

humidity The amount of water vapour in the air.

hurricane A violent storm with winds blowing at over 120 kilometres an hour.

jet stream A narrow chain of strong winds which blow at 160-320 kilometres an hour.

La Niña The change in pressure that makes the Trade winds stronger and sends cold water towards South America. The opposite to El Niño.

latitude The description used for the distance of a particular point from the Equator.

meteorologist A scientist who studies the atmosphere and predicts the weather.

monsoon Heavy rains that fall in southern Asia and central Africa.

tornado A violent, spinning column of air.

trade winds The winds that blow either side of the equator.

tropics The hot regions of the Earth either side of the Equator.

typhoon A violent storm.

water vapour Water which is in the air in the form of a gas. When the air cools, it falls as rain or snow.

Further Information

BOOKS

Air (Against the Elements series)
by S Angliss (Watts, 1998)
The Complete Book of the Earth
by A Claybourne, G Doherty and
R Treays (Usborne, 1999)
The Kingfisher Book of Planet Earth
by Martin Redfern (Kingfisher, 1999)
Restless Planet: Floods by Dr Mark
Maslin (Wayland, 1999)

CD-ROMS

Violent Earth
(Wayland Multimedia, 1997)
PC and MAC versions available.
Looks at floods, hurricanes, tornadoes
and duststorms, plus earthquakes and
volcanoes.

WEBSITES

The World Wide Web has hundreds of
sites providing information about
storms. Here are a few for you to
look at.

http://www.bgs.ac.uk/news/events/
beachy/photos.htm
This website has superb pictures of
the Beachy Head cliff collapse.

http://www.geocities.com
This website has lots of information
about tornadoes.

http://www.pmel.noaa.gov/toga-tao/el-
nino/home.html
This website will give you more
information about El Niño.

http:// www.osei.noaa.gov/
OSEIstormind.html
This website gives you the latest news
on storms around the world.

Index